Drops of Water

Ella Wheeler Wilcox

Kessinger Publishing's Rare Reprints

Thousands of Scarce and Hard-to-Find Books on These and other Subjects!

- Americana
- Ancient Mysteries
- Animals
- Anthropology
- Architecture
- Arts
- Astrology
- Bibliographies
- Biographies & Memoirs
- Body, Mind & Spirit
- Business & Investing
- Children & Young Adult
- Collectibles
- Comparative Religions
- Crafts & Hobbies
- Earth Sciences
- Education
- Ephemera
- Fiction
- Folklore
- Geography
- Health & Diet
- History
- Hobbies & Leisure
- Humor
- Illustrated Books
- Language & Culture
- Law
- Life Sciences

- Literature
- Medicine & Pharmacy
- Metaphysical
- Music
- Mystery & Crime
- Mythology
- Natural History
- Outdoor & Nature
- Philosophy
- Poetry
- Political Science
- Science
- Psychiatry & Psychology
- Reference
- Religion & Spiritualism
- Rhetoric
- Sacred Books
- Science Fiction
- Science & Technology
- Self-Help
- Social Sciences
- Symbolism
- Theatre & Drama
- Theology
- Travel & Explorations
- War & Military
- Women
- Yoga
- *Plus Much More!*

We kindly invite you to view our catalog list at:
http://www.kessinger.net

TO
THAT MOST EARNEST WORKER IN THE CAUSE OF
TEMPERANCE,
Theo. D. Ranouse,
G. W. C. Templar of Wisconsin,
WHOSE UNFLAGGING ZEAL HAS ACCOMPLISHED SO
MUCH FOR
OUR STATE,
THIS VOLUME,
IS MOST RESPECTFULLY DEDICATED BY
THE AUTHOR.

1

A GLASS OF WINE.

"What's in a glass of wine?"
　　There, set the glass where I can look within.
Now listen to me, friend, while I begin
　　And tell you what I see--
What I behold with my far-reaching eyes,
　　And what I know to be
Below the laughing bubbles that arise
　　Within this glass of wine.
There is a little spirit, night and day,
That cries one word, for ever and alway:
　　That single word is "More!"
And whoso drinks a glass of wine, drinks *him*:
You fill the goblet full unto the brim,
　　And strive to silence him.

Glass after glass you drain to quench his thirst,
Each glass contains a spirit like the first;
　　And all their voices cry
Until they shriek and clamor, howl and rave,
　　And shout "More!" noisily,
Till welcome death prepares the drunkard's grave,
　　And stills the imps that rave.

　　That see I in the wine:
And tears so many that I cannot guess;
And all these drops are labelled with "Distress."
　　I know you cannot see.
And at the bottom are the dregs of shame:
　　Oh! it is plain to me.
And there are woes too terrible to name:
　　Now drink your glass of wine.

ALCOHOL'S REQUIEM UPON PROF. P. F. K.,

A GIFTED MAN, WHO DIED A VICTIM TO STRONG DRINK

Ho! ho! Father Death! I have won you another!
  Another grand soul I have ruined and taken;
I, who am licensed by good Christian people,
  Eat and eat at their souls till by angels forsaken:
I spoil them, I soil them, and past all reclaiming
They fall, sick with sins that are too black for
naming.

Ho! ho! Father Death! count me as your best man:
  I bring you more souls than famine or battle.
Let pestilence rage! it will last but a season,
  And the soft voice of peace stills the cannon's
loud rattle;
But I, pausing never, with ceaseless endeavor,
Night and day, day and night, I am toiling for ever.

Ho! ho! Father Death! I have brought you my
thousands:
  Good people help me, license, uphold me,
Gaze on some victim I stole from their household--
  Gaze, and upbraid the foul demon that sold me.
Ah! but they helped him--argued and voted
Till *license* was granted, and I was promoted.

Ho! ho! Father Death! is he not a grand victim?
  I bring you souls that are well worth the winning--
Noble and brave, with the rare gifts of heaven;

But I eat them away and pollute them with
sinning.
Now, but for me there would be few above him,
Honored and prized by the dear ones who love him.

A MOTHER'S WAIL.

The sweet young Spring walks over the earth,
  It flushes and glows on moor and lea;
The birds are singing in careless mirth,
  The brook flows cheerily on to the sea;
And I know that the flowers are blooming now
Over my beautiful darling's brow:
Blooming and blowing in perfume now
Over my poor lost darling's brow.

The breath of the passionate Summer turns
  The green of the hills to a deeper dye;
The wind from the south land blows and burns,
  The sun grows red in the brazen sky;
And I know that the long, dank grasses wave
Over my beautiful darling's grave:
Rise and fall, and lift and wave
Over my darling's narrow grave.

The days flow on, and the summer dies,
  And glorious Autumn takes the crown;
And toward the south the robin flies,
  And the green of the hills grows dull and brown;
And the leaves, all purple, and gold, and red,
Drift over my precious darling's bed:

Drift and flutter, all gold and red,
Over my darling's lowly bed.

The Winter comes with its chilling snows,
   And wraps the world in a spotless shroud;
And cold from the north the wild wind blows,
   And the tempest rages fierce and loud;
It shrieks, and sobs, and sighs, and weeps
Over the mound where my darling sleeps:
In pity, it sobs, and sighs, and weeps
Over the mound where my lost one sleeps.

He was so young, and fair, and brave:
   The pride of my bosom--my heart's best joy;
And he lieth now in a drunkard's grave;
   My beautiful darling, my only boy:
But down in my heart of hearts, I know
He has gone where his tempters never *can* go:
To heaven his soul has gone, I know,
Where the soul of his tempters never can go.

They charmed him into their licensed hell,
   They gave him rum, and his eye grew wild;
And lower and lower down he fell,
   Till they made a fiend of my precious child:
May the curses of God fall on the soul
Who gave my darling the poison bowl!
Ay, curses dark and deep on the soul
Who tempted my darling to lift the bowl!

ARISE.

Why sit ye idly dreaming all the day,
While the golden, precious hours flit away?
See you not the day is waning, waning fast?
That the morn's already vanished in the past?

When the glowing noon approaches, we will rest
Who have worked through all the morning; but at
best,
If you work with zeal and ardor till the night,
You can only make the wasted moments right.

Think you life was made for dreaming, nothing
more,
When God's work lies all unfinished at your door?
Souls to save and hearts to strengthen--ah! such
work,
Such a richly freighted labor, who would shirk?

Then arise, O idle dreamer! Dreams are sweet,
But better flowers are growing at your feet.
If you crush, or pass unheeding, idle friend,
You shall answer for their ruin in the end.

A SIGN-BOARD.

I will paint you a sign, rumseller,
  And hang it above your door;
A truer and better sign-board
  Than ever you had before.
I will paint with the skill of a master,
  And many shall pause to see

6

This wonderful piece of painting,
  So like the reality.

I will paint yourself, rumseller,
  As you wait for that fair young boy,
Just in the morn of manhood,
  A mother's pride and joy.
He has no thought of stopping,
  But you greet him with a smile,
And you seem so blithe and friendly
  That he pauses to chat awhile.

I will paint your again, rumseller,
  I will paint you as you stand
With a foaming glass of liquor,
  Holding in either hand.
He wavers, but you urge him:
  "Drink! pledge me just this one!"
And he lifts the glass and drains it,
  And the hellish work is done.

And next I will paint a drunkard:
  Only a year has flown,
But into this loathsome creature
  The fair young boy has grown.
The work was quick and rapid:
  I will paint him as he lies,
In a torpid, drunken slumber,
  Under the winter skies.

I will paint the form of the mother,
  As she kneels at her darling's side--
Her beautiful boy, that was dearer

Than all of the world beside.
I will paint the shape of a coffin
    Labelled with one word "Lost."
I will paint all this, rumseller,
    And paint it free of cost.

The sin, and the shame and sorrow,
    The crime and sin and woe,
That is born there in your rumshop,
    No hand *can* paint, you know;
But I'll paint you a sign, rumseller,
    And many shall pause to view
This wonderful swinging sign-board,
    So terribly, fearfully true.

A TUMBLER OF CLARET.

I poured out a tumbler of Claret,
    Of course with intention to drink,
And, holding it up in the sunlight,
    I paused for a moment to think.
I really can't tell you what made me;
    I never had done so before,
Though for years, every day at my dinner,
    I had emptied one tumbler or more.

"A friend" in the loneliest hours,
    "A companion," I called the red wine,
And sometimes I poetized slightly,
    And called it a "nectar divine."
But to-day as I gazed at the claret,

That sparkled and glowed in the sun,
I asked it, "What have you done for me,
  That any true friend would have done?

"You have given me some pleasant feelings,
  But they always were followed by pain.
You have given me ten thousand headaches,
  And are ready to do it again.
You have set my blood leaping and bounding,
  Which, though pleasant, was hurtful, no doubt,
And, if I keep up the acquaintance,
  I am sure you will give me the gout.

'I remember a certain occasion,
  When you caused me to act like a fool.
And, yes, I remember another
  When you made me fall into a pool.
And there was Tom Smithers--you killed him!
  Will Howard you made a poor knave.
Both my friends! and I might count a *dozen*
  You have sent to the prison or grave.

"Is this like a loyal friend's treatment?
  And are you deserving the name?
Say! what do you give those who love you
  But poverty, sorrow, and shame?
A few paltry moments of pleasure,
  And ages of trouble and grief.
No wonder you blush in the sunlight,
  You robber, you liar, you thief!

"I will have nothing more to do with you,
  From this moment, this hour, this day.

To send you adrift, bag and baggage,
   I know is the only safe way."
And I poured out that tumbler of claret,
   Poured it *out*, and not *down*, on the spot.
And all this you see was accomplished,
   By a few sober moments of thought.

BREAKERS.

When you launch your bark for sailing
   On the sea of life, O youth!
Clothe your heart and soul and spirit
   In the blessèd garb of Truth.

Guard your every word and action:
   Never do and never say
Aught you cannot meet with pleasure
   On the mighty judgment-day.

You will meet with rocks and breakers--
   Cards and *wine* the most to fear.
Do not pause nor linger by them,
   For the devil lurketh near.

Cards and wine, the two great breakers
   That have wrecked so many souls--
Wrecked and shattered, lost to heaven,
   At the table--in the bowls.

O young man! life is before you,
   Shun the road that leads to death,

God will guide you if you ask him:
  "Seek me--here I am!" he saith.

Turn to him in all temptations,
  He will help and he will save.
When you feel your courage failing,
  He will make you strong and brave.

DON'T DRINK.

  Don't drink, boys, don't!
There is nothing of happiness, pleasure, or cheer,
In brandy, in whiskey, in rum, ale, or beer.
If they cheer you when drunk, you are certain to pay
In headaches and crossness the following day.
  Don't drink, boys, don't!

  Boys, let it alone!
Turn your back on your deadliest enemy--Drink!
An assassin disguised; nor for one moment think,
As some rashly say, that *true* women admire
The man who can boast that he's playing with fire.
  Boys, let it alone!

  No, boys, don't drink!
If the habit's begun, stop now! stop to-day!
Ere the spirit of thirst leads you on and away
Into vice, shame, and drunkenness. This is the goal,
Where the spirit of thirst leads the slave of the bowl.
  No, boys, *don't* drink!

Boys, touch not, nor taste!
Don't think you can stop at the social "First Glass."
Too many have boasted that power, alas!
And found they were slaves to this seeming good
friend,
And have grown into drunkards and knaves, in the
end.
Boys, touch not, nor taste!

Don't drink, boys, *Don't*!
If the loafers and idlers scoff, never heed:
True men and true women will wish you "God-
speed."
There is nothing of purity, pleasure, or cheer
To be gotten from whiskey, wine, brandy, or beer.
Don't drink, boys, *Don't*!

DON'T TEASE THE LION

If you saw a lion
  Not within a cage,
Would you tease and fret him
  Till he roared in rage?
Would you tempt his anger
  And his savage power,
Knowing he could crush you,
  Kill you, and devour?

Yet I know some people
  Who, morn and noon and night,
Tease and fret with *bitters*

12

The lion--appetite.
It matters not what ails them,
   For each disease and all
They seem to think there's healing
   In demon alcohol.

So they fret the lion,
   And anger him, until,
In his awful power,
   He springs up to kill.

Let me warn you, children,
   From this foolish way.
Do not tease the lion,
   Nor tempt him any day.

Don't believe the doctors
   If they say you need
Any wines or ciders;
   For there are, indeed,
Better cures, and safer,
   Than these drinks, that slay
More than a hundred people
   Without fail each day.

"GIVE US A CALL!"

[Suggested by seeing these words in a saloon advertisement.]

Give us a call! We keep good beer,
Wine, and brandy, and whiskey here;

Our doors are open to boys and men,
And even to women, now and then.
We lighten their purses, we taint their breaths,
We swell up the column of awful deaths;

    All kinds of crimes
    We sell for dimes
In our sugared poisons, so sweet to taste!
If you've money, position, or name to waste,
    Give us a call!

Give us a call! In a pint of our gin,
We sell more wickedness, shame, and sin
Than a score of clergymen, preaching all day
From dawn till darkness, could preach away,
And in our beer (though it may take longer
To get a man drunk than drinks that are stronger)
We sell out poverty, sorrow, and woe--
Who wants to purchase? Our prices are low.
    Give us a call!

Give us a call! We'll dull your brains,
We'll give you headaches and racking pains,
We'll make you old while you yet are young,
To lies and slander we'll train your tongue,
    We'll make you a shirk
    From all useful work,
Make theft and forgery seem fair play,
And murder a pastime sure to pay.
    Give us a call!

Give us a call! We are cunning and wise,
We're bound to succeed; for we advertise

In the *family papers*! the journals that claim
To be pure in morals and fair of fame.
Husbands, brothers, and sons will read
Our kind invitation, and *some* will heed
  And give us a call!
  We *pay* for all
The space in the paper we occupy.
And there's little in this life that money won't buy.

If you would go *down* in the world, and not up,
If you would be slain by the snake in the cup,
  Or lose your soul
  In the flowing bowl,
  If you covet shame
  And a blasted name,
  Give us a call!

GOD'S WORK.

TO J. J. H., OF KENTUCKY.

Gathering brands from the burning,
  Plucking them out of the fire,
Lifting the sheep that have wandered,
  Out of the dust and the mire,
Bringing home sheaves from the harvest
  To lay at the Master's feet--
Lord! all thy hosts of angels
  Must smile on a life so sweet.

Speaking with fear of no man,
   Speaking with love for all,
Warning the young and the thoughtless
   From the wild beast--"Alcohol."
Showing the snares that the tempter
   Weaveth on every hand.
Lord! all thy dear, dear angels
   Must smile on a life so grand.

Fighting the bloodless battle
   With a heart that is true and bold;
Fighting it not for glory,
   Fighting it not for gold,
But out of love for his neighbor,
   And out of love for his Lord.
And I know that the hands of the angels
   Will crown him with his reward.

For whoso works for the Master,
   And whoso fights his fight,
The angels crown with a star-wreath,
   And it glows with gems most bright.
They wear them for ever and ever,
   The saints in that land of bliss,
And I know that heaven's best jewel
   Is kept for a soul like this.

GOOD TEMPLARS' SONG.

AIR---"O SUSANNAH!"

16

Ye soldiers in the temperance cause,
  Our work is but begun.
Oh! sit not down in idleness
  And think the field is won.
Our lambs are straying from the fold,
  The wolves are on the track:
Oh! can you sit and see them go,
  Nor strive to bring them back?

Chorus: O Good Templars!
                There's work for us to-day.
            Then gird your armor on again,
              And only pause to pray.

Whichever way the eye may turn,
  It sees the rum-shop stand
With open door and flowing bowl,
  A viper in the land.
The grapes are hanging from the vines,
  All ready for the press.
Before, behind, on every side
  Are seeds of drunkenness.

Our foes are all untiring,
  But God is with the right,
And we will conquer at the last--
  Then onward to the fight!
Ay, onward to the battle-field,
  Each woman, child, and man!
King Alcohol shall yet go down
  With all his demon clan.

GREETING POEM.

[Read at the Reception of Delegates of R.W.G. Lodge
I.O.G.T.,

Madison, May 28, 1872.]

There was a sound in the wind to-day,
  Like a joyous cymbal ringing!
And the leaves of the trees talked with the breeze,
  And they altogether were singing,
For they knew that an army, both bold and strong,
  A brave, *brave* army, was coming,
Not with the fife and sounds of strife,
  With marshal music and drumming,
Not with stern faces and gleaming swords,
  That would make blood to flow like water,
While brother and brother should slay each other
  On wholesale fields of slaughter;
But rather like rills from a thousand hills,
  That ripple through valley and heather,
On, on to the sea, with a song of glee,
  Till they meet and mingle together.

They come from the South, and the East, and the
West,
  The bravest and best in the nation.
They come at no idle and aimless quest,
  But to work for a world's salvation.
From the Scot's fair land and from England's strand,
  O'er mountain and heather and ocean,
They come; and the foe by their coming shall know
  The strength of a Templar's devotion.

18

On the earnest brows, in the thoughtful eyes,
  We read the unchanging story--
They fight in their might for the truth and the right,
  And not for vain name or glory.

O grandest of armies! O bravest of bands!
  We give you a cordial greeting,
And the blood of our warm hearts beats in the hands
  That are offered to you in meeting.
The heart of a Templar is never cold,
  Nor stands it aloof from a brother,
And his hand is steady, and always ready
  To clasp the hand of another.
In God's great Book, where but angels look,
  On pages of spotless beauty
Are written in letters of living light
  A Templar's vow and his duty.
"For ever and ever," the promise reads,
  For ever and ever 'twas given.
And who keeps or breaks the pledge that he takes
  Must meet the record in heaven.

Our order is noble and grand and strong,
  And is gathering strength each hour,
And the good of the earth proclaim its worth,
  While the foe turns pale at its power.
And we of the State that men call great,
  The nation's brave "Badger" daughter,
Step by step as we go, are defeating the foe,
  While we add to the hosts of cold water.

With a chief at our head whom the foe may well
dread,

The Sherman or Grant of our battles,
By day and by night we fight the good fight,
    Though never a cannon rattles.
For the *tongue* and the *pen* are the swords of our
men,
    And prayer keeps them whetted and polished;
They will let God's light in on the foe's licensed sin,
    Till the traffic of death is abolished.

With cunning hands we fashioned the strands
    Of a stout restraining tether,
To fasten the beast, for a season at least,
    And our statesmen tied it together.
The beast strains the rope with the idle hope
    Of making it weaker or longer,
But the Templars to-day are working away
    To make it *shorter* and *stronger*.

We give you greeting--we need your aid!
    There is work for many a morrow,
There are beautiful souls going down in the bowls,
    There are homes that are burdened with sorrow,
There are mourning captives all over the earth,
    Hugging the fetters that bind them.
We must show them the light, we must set them
aright,
    We must work for them all as we find them.

With a soaring "Faith," that is stronger than death,
    We must work while the day hangs o'er us.
We are brave and strong, and our battle-song
    Has "Hope" for the ringing chorus.
With "Charity" broad as the mercy of God,

We must lift up the fallen neighbor,
And the Lord's dear band, in the angel land,
   Will smile on our blesséd labor.

Welcome, brave warriors in God's holy cause!
   The hearts in our bosoms are beating
As one heart to-night, filled with pride and delight--
   Welcome, thrice welcome, our greeting.
And though soon between will lie long miles of
green,
   Though oceans divide us for ever,
The ties which now bind heart with heart, mind with
mind,
   The hand of Death only can sever.

HAUNTED.

What are these nameless mysteries,
   These subtleties of life and death,
That bring before our spirit eyes
   The loved and lost; or, like a breath
Of lightest air, will touch the cheek,
And yet a wordless language speak?

In every breeze that blows, to-day,
   One voice seems speaking unto me;
And north or south, whichever way
   I turn my gaze, one face I see,
And closely, closely at my side
A mystic shadow seems to glide.

A motley crowd we move among,
  We surge on with the mighty mass,
And yet no one in all the throng
  Looks strangely on us as we pass.
No eye but mine own seems to see
The nameless thing that walks by me.

I cannot touch a proffered hand
  But this strange shadow glides between.
Why came he from the spirit land?
  What brought him from the world unseen?
Why am I troubled and oppressed
By the vague presence of my guest?

He was my friend! I should rejoice!
  I loved him once! Why do I fear?
And yet I shudder as his voice
  Speaks in the wind. I feel him near,
This restless spirit of the dead,
And shiver with a nameless dread.

I loved him once; he was my friend;
  He held the first place in my heart,
And might have held it to the end.
  But our two ways spread wide apart:
I kept the path upon the hill,
And he went down and down, until

He reached the depths of sin and shame,
  And died as sots and drunkards die.
I ceased to even speak his name.
  God knows I never thought that I,

Who blamed his lack of moral strength,
Might answer for his fall, at length!

O restless dead, lost friend of mine!
  I *might* have saved you, had I tried.
I saw you lift the glass of wine,
  And, seeing, had I warned you, cried,
"Touch not, taste not the drink accursed!"
I *might* have saved you from the thirst

That swallowed up your brain and soul.
  But nay! I scorned you when you fell,
And, looking upward to *my* goal,
  Left you to stagger down to hell.
Accusing spirit of the dead,
Your presence fills my heart with dread!

IF.

If wine was banished from the earth,
  How much of sorrow would be slain!
  How much of misery and pain,
If wine was nowhere on the earth!

If rum was driven from the land,
  How many tears would be unshed!
  What bitter words would be unsaid,
If rum was nowhere in the land!

If in this weary world of ours
  Foul whiskey drinks were not distilled,

How many graves would be unfilled
In this strange, weary world of ours?

If ale was nowhere to be found,
　How much of sin would never be!
　How much of woe and misery,
If ale was nowhere to be found!

Were all the liquor rivers dried,
　This earth would be an Eden land,
　With peace and joy on every hand,
Were all the liquor rivers dried.

O Heaven! speed the blessèd day,
　And send a mighty, scorching drouth,
　And dry these streams from north to south.
O Heaven! speed the blessèd day!

IF I WERE SENT.

If I were sent to represent
　A portion of a nation,
I would not chat on this and that
　In the halls of legislation.
To show my power, I'd waste no hour
　In aimless talk and bother,
Nor fritter away a precious day
　On this, and that, and the other;

Whether the food a dog consumes
　Wouldn't make a porker fatter;*

And about a thousand aimless things
   Of no import or matter;
Whether each day a man should pray*
   For our welfare or shouldn't.
Now, I do not SAY men DO this way,
   I merely say *I* wouldn't:

No! were I sent to represent
   A State, or town, or county,
I'd do some good, and all I could
   To earn the people's bounty.
Instead of a dog or a fattening hog,
   I'd talk about *men's drinking,*
And with words of fire, I would inspire
   The stolid and unthinking.

And the time that I *might* idly waste
   (I didn't say men *do* waste it),
I'd spend in pleading for my cause;
   And with tongue and pen I'd haste it
Through all the land, till a mighty band,
   With laws and legislation,
Should cleanse the stain, and cut the chain
   That binds our helpless nation.

And little need would there be then,
   When that bright sun had risen,
Of asylum wings or building sites,
   Of county or State prison.
The need is *made* by the liquor trade!
   O ye wise, sage law-makers!
'Tis the fiend you smile upon that makes
   Our madmen and law-breakers.

"Two-thirds"--so reads our State Report--
  Are made insane through liquor.
And so I say, I'd spend no day
  In idle talk or bicker,
If I were sent to represent
  A portion of a nation;
But I'd plead for laws, until my cause
  Was won through legislation.

*A certain legislative body spent hours in
discussing such trivial matters.

IN MEMORIAM.

[A tribute to the memory of Thurlow W Brown, who devoted
his life to the cause of temperance, and whose truly
marvellous labors and sacrifices for that cause are but half
understood or appreciated.]

Looking some papers over,
  Dusty and dim and old,
I found some words that thrilled me
  With their ring of genuine gold--
Words that were better than rubies,
  And they stirred me even to tears,
For the hand that wrote them has rested
  Under the sod for years.

O name to be spoken softly!
  O sainted Thurlow Brown!
The world lost one of its heroes
  When he dropped the cross for the crown.

And the cause he loved and fought for
 Lost more than my tongue can tell
For he left no soul behind him
 That could do the work so well.

When I think of his mighty labors,
 My own seem weak and vain,
And I know that his place in the vineyard
 Can never be filled again.
But the burning words that he uttered,
 Or that dropped like coals from his pen,
Shall live for ever and ever
 In the hearts and minds of men.

O God! if spirits do ever
 Come down from heaven on high,
Let the spirit of this great hero
 Sometimes be hovering nigh;
And give him the power to guide us
 In all that we do or say
For the cause he loved and fought for.
 Oh! grant it, Lord, I pray.

IN THE CUP.

There is grief in the cup!
I saw a proud mother set wine on the board;
The eyes of her son sparkled bright as she poured
The ruddy stream into the glass in his hand.
The cup was of silver; the lady was grand
In her satins and laces; her proud heart was glad

In the love of her fair, noble son; but, oh! sad,
Oh! *so* sad ere a year had passed by,
And the soft light had gone from her beautiful eye.
For the boy that she loved, with a love strong as
death,
In the chill hours of morn with a drunkard's foul
breath
And a drunkard's fierce oath, reeled and staggered
his way
To his home, a dark blot on the face of the day.

There is shame in the cup!
The tempter said, "Drink," and a fair maiden
quaffed
Till her cheeks glowed the hue of the dangerous
draught.
The voice of the tempter spoke low in her ear
Words that once would have started the quick,
angry tear,
But wine blunts the conscience, and wine dulls the
brain,
She listened and smiled, and he whispered again.
He lifted the goblet: "Once more," he said, "drink,"
And the soul of the maiden was lost in the brink.

There is death in the cup!
A man in God's image, strong, noble, and grand,
With talents that crowned him a prince of the land,
Sipped the ruddy red wine!--sipped it lightly at first,
Until from its chains broke the demon of thirst.
And thirst became master, and man became slave,
And he ended his life in the drunkard's poor grave.
Wealth, fame, talents, beauty, and life swallowed

up,
Grief, shame, death, destruction, are *all* in the cup.

IN THE NIGHT.

In the silent midnight watches,
  When the earth was clothed in gloom,
And the grim and awful darkness
  Crept unbidden to my room--
On the solemn, deathly stillness
  Of the night, there broke a sound,
Like ten million wailing voices
  Crying loudly from the ground.

From ten million graves came voices,
  East and West, and North and South,
Leagues apart, and yet together
  Spake they, e'en as with one mouth:
"Men and women! men and women!"
  Cried these voices from the ground,
And the very earth was shaken
  With the strange and awful sound--

"Ye who weep in selfish sorrow,
  Ye who laugh in selfish mirth,
Hark! and listen for a moment
  To the voices from the earth:
Wake and listen! ye who slumber,
  Pause and listen! ye who feast,
To the warning of the voices
  From the graves in West and East.

"We, the victims of a demon,
  We, who one, and each, and all,
Can cry out before high heaven,
  'We are slain by alcohol!'--
We would warn you, youths and maidens,
  From the path that we have trod--
From the path that leads *to* ruin,
  And *away* from peace and God.

"We, the millions who have fallen,
  Warn you from the ruddy glow
Of the wine in silver goblets,
  For *destruction* lies below.
Wine and gin, and rum and brandy,
  Whiskey, cider, ale, and beer,
These have slain us and destroyed us--
  These the foes that brought us here.

"'You are safe,' you say. Ah heaven!
  So *we* said, and drank, and died.
'We are safe!' we proudly boasted,
  Yet we sank down in the tide.
There is never any safety
  From the snares of alcohol
For the youth who looks on liquor,
  Tastes or touches it at all.

"We beseech you, men and women,
  Fathers, mothers, sons, and wives,
To arise, and slay the demon
  That is threatening dear ones' lives!
Do not preach of *moderation*
  To your children; for, alas!

There is not a foe more subtle
  Than the fateful 'social glass.'

"Thoughtless mother, wife, or sister,
  Dash that poison cup away!
He, the husband, son, or brother
  Who so gaily sips to-day,
May to-morrow stagger homeward,
  Jeered and scorned by sober men.
Would you smile upon him proudly--
  Would you say, 'I did it,' then?

"Ah! a vast and mighty number
  Of the drunkards in all lands
Take the first step to destruction
  Led by white and fragile hands.
Every smile you give the wine-cup,
  Every glance, O lady fair!
Like a spade, digs down and hollows out
  A drunkard's grave somewhere.

"Men in office, men in power,
  Will you let this demon wild
Stalk unfettered through the nation,
  Slaying woman, man, and child?
Oh! arouse, ye listless mortals,
  There is work for every one!
We have warned you of your danger--
  We have spoken, we have done."

Round about me fell the silence
  Of the solemn night once more,
And I heard the quiet ticking

Of the clock outside my door.
It was not a dreamer's fancy,
    Not a romance of my brain,
But the warning of the victims
    That old Alcohol had slain.

IS IT BEST?

O mother who sips sweetened liquors!
    Look down at the child on your breast;
Think, think of the rough path before him,
    And ask yourself then, "Is it best?
Shall I foster a love for this poison,
    Instil the thirst into *his* veins?
In the fountain he seeks at my bosom
    Sow the rank seeds of death, grief, and pains?

"Shall I give him the thirst of the drunkard,
    Bequeath him the weapons of crime?
Can we look for a glass of pure water
    Dipped up from a fountain of slime?
Can we look for brave men, strong and noble,
    Where the parents drink poison for food?
When the body and soul are corrupted,
    Can we look for the *works* to be good?"

Oh! think of the future before him!
    There are perils you cannot remove.
Yet this, the great highway of sorrow--
    Oh! guard him from *this* with your love.
There are rough paths enough in the future

For the feet of the child on your breast;
And lower the glass you are lifting,
    And ask yourself, then, "Is it best?"

IS IT WELL?

Saw you the youth, with the face like the morning,
    Refilling the glass, that foamed white as the sea?
Heard you the words that fell down like a warning,
    "Lift not the glass: it holds sorrow for thee"?
        He heeds not nor listens:
        The red liquor glistens,
And he sees not the fangs of the serpent beneath.
        And the fiends are elated,
        And the voice waileth "Fated,"
As he drains out the glass: the dumb agent of death.

High had he set his mark. Fame, wealth, and glory,
    All should be his ere the noon-tide of life.
A name that should live in the annals of story,
    His was a heart that could battle with strife.
        "Here's to youthful endeavor!"
        He cries. "Ah! for ever
Shall the ruddy glass cheer me on life's rugged way.
        There is strength for all trouble
        In each airy bubble.
Who dares prate of danger and sorrow, I pray?"

Where is the youth with the face like the morning?
    Where are the hopes that glowed bright as the
noon!

33

He who had heard and obeyed not the warning,
Oh! has he reaped the dire harvest so soon?
He quaffed, all unheeding
The small voice's pleading,
And he lieth to-night in a dark prison cell.
This is his glory,
The name carved in story.
This has the red glass done. Say, is it well?

MASTER AND SERVANT.

The devil to Bacchus said, one day,
In a scowling, growling, petulant way,
As he came from earth to hell:
"There's a soul above that I cannot move,
And I've struggled long and well;
He's a manly youth, with an eye of truth,
A fellow of matchless grace;
And he looks me through with his eye of blue
Till I cower before his face.
The very power and strength of heaven
To this young, fearless soul were given;
For I've never an art that can reach his heart,
And I cannot snare his feet:
I have wasted days in devising ways,
And now must cry 'Defeat!'"
And the devil scowled, and grumbled, and growled,
And beat about with his cane,
Till the demons fled over the burning waste
Out of his reach in hurrying haste,
Howling aloud in pain.

Bacchus laughed as he stooped and quaffed
    A burning bumper of wine:
"Why, master," said he, "you soon shall see
    The fellow down at your shrine;
Long ago, if you'd let me know,
    We'd had him in our ranks.
And now, adieu! while I work for you;
    Don't hurry about your thanks!
I'm going above; you know they love
    The sight of my glowing face.
They call me a *god*! ho! ho! how odd!
    With *this* for my dwelling-place."

A youth with a dower of manly grace,
A maid with the morning in her face;
And she filleth a goblet full to the brim,
And giveth the bubbling draught to him.
"Drink!" she says, and the goblet sways
    And shimmers under his eyes.
He tries to speak, but the tongue is weak,
    And the words sink into sighs;
For the maid is fair, and she holds him there
    With a spell that he cannot flee:
"Drink!" and she sips with her ruby lips--
    "Drink but a draught with me."
And the lovers quaffed, while the demons laughed,
    And Bacchus laughed loud and long.
"Ho! ho!" cried he, "what a victory!
    Ho! ho! for the soul so strong
That my master was beat, and cried 'Defeat!'
But wine is a tempter, and love is sweet."

Bacchus went back o'er the fiery track
  Into the land below;
And the devil said, "Well, what have you to tell
  Of the thing I want to know?"

And Bacchus said he, "Why, look and see!
  There is your strong, brave youth
Reeling along, with a drunken song
  Staining those lips of truth.
My work is done! You must go on
  And finish the job I started;
And as long as I stay in your service, pray,
  Don't ever be down-hearted."

NATIONAL ANNIVERSARY ODE.

Ho! for the day in the whole year the brightest!
  Long may it live in the heart of the nation!
Long may it be ere the names are forgotten
  That boldly were signed to the grand declaration!
Shout, sons of liberty! shout for the one land free
    Under the sun!
On this thrice blessèd day its bonds were struck
away,
    Its thongs undone!

Ho! for our banner, the emblem of freedom!
  What can arouse a true hero's devotion--
What like the Stars and Stripes, floating above us?
  Queen of all lands, and the peer of the ocean.
Oh! it is fair to see, oh! it is dear to me,

Flag of the brave!
Time's wheel shall cease to move, true hearts shall
cease to love,
    Ere it cease to wave.

But there's a blemish now staining our banner!
    The bright stars are dimmed, and the fair stripes
are spotted,
    With the tears of the drunkard's wife, mother, and
children,
    With hot tears of shame is our flag blurred and
blotted.
Victims of tyranny, *strike* till our land is free
    From King Alcohol;
Strike down his whelps of sin, rum, brandy, beer,
and gin
    Strangle them all.

Up to the contest, and wipe out this blemish!
    Columbia's son, and Columbia's daughter,
    God speed the day when the one "Land of
Freedom"
    Shall add to its title the "Land of Cold Water"!
Three cheers for Columbia, and this, her natal day!
    God bless the right,
And guard from a traitor's hand, this our beloved
land,
    And the Red, Blue, and White!

July 4th, 1871.

NEW YEAR.

The New Year dawns again upon the earth,
And all our land re-echoes with its mirth.
From east to west, from north to south, we hear
The sounds of merriment and goodly cheer--
With feast and revelry, with dance and song,
The golden hours slip happily along,
And eyes are bright, and hearts are blithe and gay,
And all seems well upon this New Year Day.

Alas! alas! all is not well; for, oh!
White hands will plant the seeds of sin and woe--
Fair maids, with smiles and glances half divine,
Will lift the muddy glass of poison wine
To manly lips, and plead of them to quaff,
And loud will grow the careless jest and laugh;
And firm resolves, that gird up manly hearts
To brave the devil and withstand his arts,
Will fail before these fiends in forms so sweet,
And they will drain the glass and think it meet.

O shame too deep for tongue or pen to tell!
That woman opens wide the door of hell
For man to enter--woman, who should be
As true as truth and pure as purity.

But when they pass the drunkard in the street,
They lift their robes, lest they shall touch his feet,
And turn from him with scornful eye and lip,
Forgetting that perchance some maiden bade him
sip--
Bade him with thrilling glance and tender tone,

Until the deadly habit, mighty grown,
Had mastered all his manhood, and he fell
Lower and lower to the depths of hell.

Go shout aloud fair woman's shame, O wind!
Tell it to nature, and to all mankind,
To hill and vale, and every forest tree,
To bird and beast, and to the mighty sea;
And let them all unite and sing her shame,
Until, with streaming eyes and cheeks aflame,
She makes a vow, and calls on God to hear,
That evermore her record shall be clear,
And she, with all her strength, will strive to save
Instead of aiding to the drunkard's grave.

OLDER THAN YOU.

We are younger in *years*! Yes, that is true;
But in *some* things we are older than you.
For instance, you sometimes say with a smile,
"It will do to drink wine once in a while."
We say, "It will not do *at all*!"
Wine is an imp of old Alcohol.
So are gin and beer, and cider, too.
If you drink up *them*, they will eat up *you*.

"*Cider* is not a strong drink," you say.
Ah! but, my friend, it opens the way
For brandy and whiskey to follow fast.
It has done it many a time in the past.
It tempts and teases the appetite.

Let it alone, boys, keep to the right;
Onward and upward we mean to go.
Heaven is reached that way, you know.

People who drink are behind the time.
They are back with darkness, and woe, and crime.
This age is *progressive*. You people who drink,
Though ever so little, just pause and *think*--
Think of the anguish that liquor makes;
Think of the hearts that it burdens and breaks.
Let it alone: stop drinking *to-day*--
This is what we, the children, say.

"ONE WAS TAKEN, AND ONE WAS LEFT."

Two harvesters walked through the rows of corn,
Down to the ripe wheat fields, one morn.
Both were fair, in the flush of youth,
With hearts of courage and eyes of truth--
Fair and young, with the priceless wealth
Of strength, and beauty, and glowing health.

Loud and clear was their mellow song
On the morning air, as they strode along.
And the reaper clashed on its yellow track,
And the song of the driver answered back
To the harvesters, as they bound the wheat
That sheaf on sheaf lay at their feet.

High rose the sun o'er the golden plain,
And the binders rested by the grain,
And sitting there, 'neath a friendly shade,
Each quenched the thirst that their labor made;
But one drank from the water mug,
And the other from the whiskey jug.

Back to their tasks went the binders twain,
Binding the sheaves of the yellow grain,
On sped the reaper, to and fro
Slaying the wheat with a cruel blow,
Leaving it slaughtered, rank on rank--
And again the binders paused and drank.

Higher and hotter rose the sun:
On sped the moments, one by one--
And again the binders stopped and quaffed
From the mug and the jug a cooling draught.
And slowly, slowly they bound the wheat
As the sun shone down with its scorching heat.

Slower, still slower, one youth goes round:
He falls--he lieth upon the ground.
A cry for help, and the workmen come
And carry their stricken comrade home.
"And one is taken, and one is left."
Weepeth the mother, "I am bereft."

One youth alone, on another morn,
Walks to the field through the rows of corn.
He who drank of the sparkling tide
Walketh still in his manhood's pride;

But he who drank from the jug lies low,
Dead, in the morn of his manhood's glow.

ONE WOMAN'S MEMORY.

Here is a lock of his soft, dark hair,
  And here are the letters he wrote to me.
And the ring of gold that I used to wear
  Is here in the casket--see!
I put them away ten years ago.
  "What is it," you ask, "did I love in vain?
Was my lover unfaithful?" No, oh! no.
  My heart was spared *that* pain.

He died in the bloom of his manhood's youth.
  You say I have his memory, friend;
That he is not dead, but lives, in truth;
  Wait till you hear the end.
Death in itself is a little thing,
  It is only passing from *here* to *there*;
But a death of *shame* has a bitter sting
  That makes it hard to bear.

He was good and true as a man could be,
  Noble and pure, when I loved him first;
But all of his race were cursed, you see,
  With a fiery, craving thirst.
And the tempter, morning and noon and night,
  Was placed in his path by a mother's hand.
The woe of wine, and its blasting blight,
  She did not understand.

I did not know, or I did not think,
  Of the awful shame that was hidden there
When I saw him lift the glass, and drink
  To the health of his "lady fair."
I knew and I thought when it was too late.
  I reached out my hands, but I could not save.
He hurried on to his fearful fate,
  And sank in a drunkard's grave.

He was good, and kind, and true, but *weak*
  When the ruby wine danced o'er the brim.
And woe is me that I did not speak
  One warning word to him!
If I had but told him to cast away,
  To touch not and taste not the mocker, wine,
I need not have felt as I feel to-day
  That *blood* stains these hands of mine.

O ye who have friends on the awful brink
  That hangs o'er the river of ruin and death!
When you see them lift the glass, oh! think
  Of the jaggèd rocks beneath.
Reach out a hand ere the deed is done.
  Send forth a cry in the dear Lord's name.
Oh! stand not aloof while a precious one
  Speeds down to a grave of shame.

ORIGIN OF THE LIQUOR DEALER.

The devil in hell gave a festival,
  And he called his imps from their wine--

Called them up from the ruddy cup,
  And marshalled them into line.
And each to his place sprang the imps apace,
  And they stood there, side by side.
"Now, listen well, O ye hosts of hell!
  And mark me," the devil cried.

"There is work to do for all of you,
  Held for this night in store.
Then stir up the fire, till it burneth higher
  Than ever it burned before.
When the coals glow hot, set ye the pot
  Half full of the best brimstone.
And three of the worst and the most accursed
  Hell claimeth as its own
Of demons bring, when the pot shall sing,
  And cast them into the boil."
Then over the region scattered the legion
  Away to the fiendish toil.

They work with a will, and they work until
  Three imps are aboil in the pot;
And the devil stands, and stirs with his hands
  The liquid, seething hot;
And the demons revel around the devil
  With many a fiendish shout,
Till he cries "Ho, ho!" and the demons go
  And turn the liquid out.

Turn it in, to a lake of gin,
  Where the devil bathes, to cool.
Then lift it up, and turn on a cup
  Of wine they dip from a pool.

Then they dip it in ale, till it turneth pale,
　　In beer, till it gloweth red.
It? nay, HE! for the thing they see
　　Is a *man*, from heel to head.

And he clasps the hands of the devil who stands
　　Bowing before his face.
And he says, "Dear friend, will you please to send
　　A lad to show me my place?"

And the devil winks sly: and he says, "Ay, ay!"
　　Old fellow, I guess you'll do.
You can work more wrong with that oily tongue
　　Than all my malicious crew.

"You must go to the earth! In th' halls of mirth,
　　In the teeming city's heart--
In any place that you show your face
　　I will help you do your part.

I will give you a name--it is steeped in shame,
　　But the world will use you well.
It is 'Liquor Dealer.' It means *soul stealer*
　　And Major-General of Hell.
Go forth, my friend, and work to the end,
　　I will pay you in gleaming gold;
For every soul you drown in the bowl,
　　I will give you wealth untold."

Then forth he went, this fiend hell-sent,
　　And he doeth his work to-day--
Doeth it well; and the hosts of hell
　　Are singing his praise alway.

OUT OF THE DEPTHS.

WRITTEN AFTER THE REFORMATION OF A
BRILLIANT AND TALENTED MAN.

Out of the midnight, rayless and cheerless,
  Into the morning's golden light;
Out of the clutches of wrong and ruin,
  Into the arms of truth and right;
Out of the ways that are ways of sorrow,
  Out of the paths that are paths of pain,
Yea, out of the depths has a soul arisen,
  And "one that was lost is found again."

Lost in the sands of an awful desert,
  Lost in the region of imps accursed,
With bones of victims to mark his pathway,
  And burning lava to quench his thirst;
Lost in the darkness, astray in the shadows;
  Father above, do we pray in vain?
Hark! on the winds come gleeful tidings,
  Lo! he was lost, but is found again.

Found! and the sunlight of God's great mercy
  Dispels the shadows, and brings the morn.
Found! and the hosts of the dear Redeemer
  Are shouting aloud o'er a soul new born,
Plucked, like a brand, from the conflagration,
  Cleansed, like a garment, free from stain,
Saved, pray God, for ever and ever;
  Lost for a season, but found again.

"Out of the depths" by the grace of heaven,
  Out of the depth of woe and shame,

And he blots his name from the roll of drunkards,
  To carve it again on the heights of fame.
"Wine is a mocker, and strong drink raging."
  Glory to God, he has snapped the chain
That bound him with fetters of steel and iron,
  And he that he was lost is found again.

Down with the cup, though it gleam like rubies;
  Down with the glass, though it sparkle and shine,
"It bites like a serpent, and stings like an adder,"
  There is woe, and sorrow, and shame in wine.
Keen though the sword be, and deadly its mission,
  Three times its number the wine-cup has slain.
God, send thy grace unto those it has fettered--
  God, grant the lost may be found again.

"PH. BEST & CO.'S LAGER-BEER."

In every part of the thrifty town,
  Whether my course be up or down,
In lane, and alley, and avenue,
Painted in yellow, and red, and blue,
This side and that, east and west,
Was this flaunting sign-board of "Ph. Best."

'Twas hung high up, and swung in the air
With a swaggering, bold-faced, "devil-may-care-
It-is-none-of-your-business" sort of way;
Or, as if dreading the light o' the day,
It hung low, over a basement-stair,
And seemed ashamed when you saw it there.

Or it shone like a wicked and evil eye
From a "restaurant" door on passers-by,
And seemed with a twinkling wink to say:
"Are you bound for hell? Then step this way;
This is the ticket-office of sin;
If you think of purchasing, pray, walk in."

Or it glared from a window where the light
Of the lamps within shone full and bright,
And seemed to be saying, "Come out of the storm!
Come into my haven snug and warm;
I will give you warmth from the flowing bowl,
And all I ask is your purse and soul."

But whether on window, door, or stair,
Wherever I went, it was always *there*;
Painted in yellow, and red, and blue,
It stared from alley and avenue:
It was north, and south, and east, and west,
The lager-beer of this Philip Best.

And who was Philip Best, you ask?
Oh! he was a man, whose noble task
Was the brewing of beer--good beer, first-class--
That should sparkle, and bubble, and boil in the
glass:
Should sparkle and flow till drank, and then
Feast like a vampire on brains of men.

Ah! Philip Best, you have passed from view,
But your name and your works live after you.
Come, brothers, raise him a monument,
Inscribed, "Here lies the man who sent

A million of souls to the depths of hell;
Turned genius and worth to the prison-cell;

Stole bread from the mouth of the hungry child:
Made the father a brute, and the mother wild;
Filled happy homes with dread unrest:
Oh! a very great man was Philip Best.
O Ph. Best! you have passed from view,
But your *name* and your *deeds* live after you."

SLAIN.

Hollow a grave where the willows wave,
  And lay him under the grasses,
Where the pitying breeze bloweth up from the seas,
  And murmurs a chant as it passes.

Lay the beautiful face and the form of grace
  Away from the gaze of mortal.
Let us hope that his soul has gained the goal
  Over the shining portal.

Hope! Ah! we thrill with a terrible chill.
  Ah! pen, can you tell the story
Of the one who died in his manhood's pride,
  Slain in the morn of his glory?

There's a blemish of shame on the dear one's name,
  For he died as the drunkard dieth.
The ruddy wine-mug was the fiend who dug
  The grave where our darling lieth.

O God! and his soul, was it lost in the bowl?
  Has it gone where the wicked goeth?
Shall *he* bear the sin, and the tempter go in
  Where the beautiful city gloweth?

Hush! O my heart! act well thy part,
  Nor question a Father's kindness,
And strive not to see the thing hid from thee
  By a veil of earthly blindness.

But all through the wine may there shimmer and
shine,
  As it glimmers and glows in the glasses,
A coffin and grave, and the willows that wave
  Over our dead 'neath the grasses.

THANKSGIVING.

[Written after the passage of the Temperance Law in
Wisconsin, 1872.]

Thank God for *men*! I hear the shout
From East and West go up and out.
Thank God for men whose hearts are true;
For men who boldly *dare* and *do*;
For men who are not bought and sold,
Who value honor more than gold;
For men large-hearted, noble-minded;
For men whose visions are not blinded
With selfish aims--men who will fight
With tongue or sword for what is right;
For men whom threats can never cower;

For men who dare to use their power
To shield the right and punish wrong,
E'en though his hosts are bold and strong
For men who work with hearts and hands
For what the public good demands.
Bless God! the thankful people say,
Such men have not *all* passed away.

Bless God enough are left at least
To put a muzzle on the beast
That walks our land from breadth to length
And robs the strong man of his strength;
Takes bread from babes, steal wise men's brains,
And leaves them bound in helpless chains;
Makes sin and sorrow, shame and woe,
Wherever his cloven feet may go.
This is the mission of the beast
Whose bloated keepers sit and feast
On seasoned dainties, that were bought
With blood, and tears, and God knows what--
Keepers who laugh when women cry,
Who smile when children starve and die,
If so they gain one farthing more
To add to their ill-gotten store.

From South and North, from West and East,
The people clamored, "Chain the beast!
Fetter the monster Alcohol
Before he robs us of our all."

Thank God the earnest cry was heard,
And hearts of noble men were stirred.
And though a weak-kneed host went down

Before the keeper's threatening frown,
Enough *were* left, a bold, brave few,
Strong-brained, broad-souled men who were true--
Men who were men, and did not fear
The villain's threat or coward's sneer;
Enough to muzzle with the law
The foulest beast the world ever saw.
Thank God! thank God! the people say,
True men have not *all* passed away.

THE BLACK CHARGER.

There's a terrible steed that rests not night nor day,
But onward and onward, for ever away,
Through hamlet, through village, through country,
through town,
Is heard the dread thud of his hoofs beating down;
Is seen the fierce eye, is felt the hot breath;
And before it, behind it, spreads ruin and death:
By castle, by cottage, by hut, and by hall,
Still faster and fiercer he passes them all.

He breathes on the youth with the face of the morn,
He leaves him a mark for the finger of scorn;
He cries, "Mount and ride! I will bear you away
To the fair fields of pleasure. Come, mount me, I
say!"
And, alas for the youth! he is borne like the wind,
And he leaveth his manhood, his virtue, behind;
And faster, still faster, he speeds down the track,
Where many shall follow, and few shall come back.

He breathes on the heart that is stricken with grief:
"Come, mount me! and fly to the plains of relief.
I will bear you away to the fair fields elysian,
Where your sorrows shall seem but a long-vanished
vision.
With the future before you, forgetting the past,
You shall revel in pleasure, rejoicing at last."
Ah! whoso shall mount shall ride to his doom:
Shall be sunk in the marshes of terror and gloom.

He breathes on the king, and he breathes on the
slave;
On the young and the old from the crib to the grave;
On masterly minds, and they wither away
As the flower droops and dies 'neath a torrid sun's
ray;
On beautiful souls that are pure as the light,
And they shrivel, polluted with mildew and blight:
The master, the servant, the high and the low,
He bears them *all* down to the regions of woe.

Ho! ho! temperance clan! rest ye not night nor day:
Watch, watch for the steed! starve him down! block
his way!
Throw him into the dust! seize his long, flowing
mane!
Bind his terrible limbs till he quivers in pain.
Stab him through to the heart! beat him down till he
lies
Stark and stiff on the earth--beat him down till he
dies!
Till never by castle, by cottage, by hall,
Shall again pass the black-hearted steed, Alcohol!

THE BREWER'S DOG.

The brewer's dog is abroad, boys,
   Be careful where you stray,
His teeth are coated with poison,
   And he's on the watch for prey.
The brewery is his kennel,
   But he lurks on every hand,
And he seeks for easy victims
   The children of the land.

His eyes gleam through the windows
   Of the gay saloon at night,
And in many a first-class "drug-store"
   He is hiding out of sight.
Be careful where you enter,
   And, if you smell his breath,
Flee as you would from a viper,
   For its fumes are the fumes of death.

O boys! would you kill the bloodhound?
   Would you slay the snarling whelp?
I know that you can do it
   If every one will help.
You must make a solemn promise
   To drink no ale or beer,
And soon the feeble death-wail
   Of the brewer's dog we'll hear.

For, if *all* keep the promise,
   You can starve him out, I know;
But, if boys and men keep drinking,
   The dog will thrive and grow.

THE CRY OF THE PEOPLE.

Fire! Fire! Fire! the cry rang out on the night air,
The roving winds caught it up, and the very heavens resounded.
Louder and louder still, by voices grown hoarse with terror,
The cry went up and out and a nation stood still to listen.

"Come, for the love of God, and help us fight the demon!
Come and help us to chain the fiend that is making us homeless:
His hot and scorching breath has melted our hard-earned fortunes,
And, not contented with this, he is snatching our loved ones from us.

The air is thick with the stream that pours in clouds from his nostrils:
Come, for the love of God, and help us to fetter or slay him."

The ear of the Nation heard, the heart of the Nation responded:
The smith left anvil and forge, and hastened to render assistance;
The clergyman went from the pulpit, the lawyer went from his office,
The houses of trade were closed, and a Nation was in commotion.
For the hungry tongue of Fire was lapping the skirts

of the city,
The royal Queen of the West, and her people were
crying in anguish.

Nobly and well they worked, till they chained and
fettered the demon,
Bound him hand and foot, and hindered his work of
destruction.

Over the land on wires, over the mighty cable,
Flashed the terrible truth: "Ruin and destitution
Reigns where but yesterday there was lavish wealth
and plenty."
And up from the South came aid, and aid came
down from the Northland,
And it came from East and West, wholesome food
for the hungry,
Shelter for houseless heads, and clothes to cover the
naked.

Hark! there's a sound abroad, like the cry of a
suffering people,
Loud and louder it swells, and echoes from ocean to
ocean,
The raving winds catch it up, and from throats that
are hoarse with crying
The wail goes up and out, but is answered only by
echoes.

"Come for the love of God, and help us to fetter the
demon
That is taking the bread from our mouths, and the
mouths of our helpless children;

He is walking abroad in the land, and all things
perish before him:
Homesteads crumble away, and fortunes vanish like
snow wreaths;
And, not contented with this, he is slaying our best
and our fairest,
Stealing the brains of the wise, and bringing the
young to the gallows;
He is making the home forlorn, and crowding the
jails and the prisons,
He moves the hand of the thief--*he* drives the
assassin's dagger."

The ear of the Nation is deaf, the heart of the Nation
is hardened:
The smith at his anvil and forge sings in the midst
of his labor;
The clergyman stands in his pulpit, and prays for
the soul of the sinner,
But says no word of the fiend who wrecked and
ruined the mortal;
The lawyer smokes his cigar or sips his glass of
Burgundy;
The merchant, day after day, thinks only of buying
and selling.

And up and down through the land, night and day,
walks the demon,
Poverty, sorrow, and shame follow the print of his
footsteps.
The cry of the people goes up, a cry of anguish and
pleading,
But only a few respond, a few too feeble to chain

him.
The multitude stands aloof, or aids the fiend of
destruction,
While he tramples under his hoofs hundreds and
thousands of victims--
And the multitude's ear is deaf to the wail of the
beggared orphans.

Shame, oh! shame to the Nation that leaves the
demon of Traffic
Free to roam through the land, and pillage and rob
the helpless.

Shame to the multitude that will not render
assistance,
But leaves a few to do what many can only
accomplish.

Arouse! ye listless hosts! and answer the suffering
people!
Spring to the aid of the million, as ye sprang to the
aid of the thousand:
As you fettered the demon Fire, fetter the demon
Traffic,
Who slays his tens of thousands, where the other
slew only hundreds.

THE DIRGE OF THE WINDS

The four winds of earth, the North, South, East, and
West,

Shrieked and groaned, sobbed and wailed, like the
soul of unrest.
I stood in the dusk of the twilight alone,
And heard them go by with a terrible moan.
"What is it, O winds! that is grieving you so?
Come tell me your sorrow, and tell me your woe!"
"What is it?" I questioned. They shuddered, and
said:
"We mourn for the dead! Oh! we mourn for the
dead--

"For the dishonored dead that the wine-cup has
slain;
For the wrecks that are lying on hill and on plain;
For the beautiful faces, so young and so fair,
That are lying down under the green grasses there;
For the masterful minds and beautiful souls
That were shattered, and drowned, and debased in
the bowls;
For the graves that are scattered broadcast o'er the
land,
The graves that were dug by King Alcohol's hand.
For the scenes that we saw, as we came on our way,
The sights and the sounds that degraded the day.
East and West, North and South, the tale is the
same--
A tale of debasement, and sorrow, and shame.
And this is our sorrow, and this is our woe:
It is this, it is this, that is grieving us so."

Three winds hushed their voices. The East wind
alone
Told her tale in a moaning and sorrowful tone:

"I came yesterday, from the great Eastern land,
Where the mountains are high and the cities are
grand;
But the devil walks there, night and day, in the
streets,
And he offers red wine to each soul that he greets.
They drink, and the record of crimes and of sins,
And the record of shame and of sorrow begins.
I sped from the sin-burdened East to the West,
But I find not of balm for my agonized breast.

Wine blackens the West as it blackens the East."
And the voice of the wind sobbed and wailed as it
ceased.

"I come from the West!" another voice cried,
"Where the rivers are broad, and the prairies are
wide.
There is vigor and strength in that beautiful land,
But the devil walks there with a bowl in his hand,
And the strongest grow weak, and the mightiest fall,
In the damnable reign of this King Alcohol."

He ceased, and another came mournfully forth,
And spake: "I came from the land of the North,
Where the streamlets are ice and the hillocks are
snow,
And little of passions in mortal veins flow.
But the devil walks there in that land, day and night,
And he covers his face with a mask that is white;
And he smiles as he pours out the wine for his prey,
Nor counts up the legions he kills every day."

The voice of the South wind spoke now in a sigh:
"And I, too, can tell of the thousands that die
By the hand of this king, in my soft, southern clime,
Where the sweet waters flow in a musical chime.
The devil walks there by King Alcohol's side,
And he pours out the wine till it flows in a tide;
It rushes along with a gurgling sound,
And thousands are caught in the current and
drowned."

Again the four winds cried aloud in their woe:
"It is this, it is this, that is grieving us so.
We see the mad legions go down to the grave,
Unable to warn them, unable to save,
We shriek and we groan, we shudder in pain,
For the souls that are lost, for the youths that are
slain;
And the river flows onward, the river wine-red,
And we mourn for the dead, oh! we mourn for the
dead."

THE LODGE-ROOM.

Don't bring into the lodge-room
   Anger, and spite, and pride.
Drop at the gate of the temple
   The strife of the world outside.
Forget all your cares and trials,
   Forget every selfish sorrow,
And remember the cause you meet for,
   And haste ye the glad to-morrow.

61

Drop at the gate of the temple
   Envy, and spite, and gloom.
Don't bring personal quarrels
   And discord into the room.
Forget the slights of a sister,
   Forget the wrongs of a brother,
And remember the new commandment,
   That ye all love one another.

Bring your heart into the lodge-room,
   But leave yourself outside,
That is, your personal feelings,
   Ambition, vanity, pride.
Centre each thought and power
   On the cause for which you assemble,
Fetter the demon liquor,
   And make ye the traffic tremble.

Ay! to fetter and to chain him,
   And cast him under our feet,
This is the end we aim at,
   The object for which we meet.
Then don't bring into the lodge-room,
   Envy, or strife, or pride,
Or aught that will mar our union,
   But leave them all outside.

THE LODGE-ROOM.

Don't bring into the lodge-room
   Anger, and spite, and pride.

Drop at the gate of the temple
   The strife of the world outside.
Forget all your cares and trials,
   Forget every selfish sorrow,
And remember the cause you meet for,
   And haste ye the glad to-morrow.

Drop at the gate of the temple
   Envy, and spite, and gloom.
Don't bring personal quarrels
   And discord into the room.
Forget the slights of a sister,
   Forget the wrongs of a brother,
And remember the new commandment,
   That ye all love one another.

Bring your heart into the lodge-room,
   But leave yourself outside,
That is, your personal feelings,
   Ambition, vanity, pride.
Centre each thought and power
   On the cause for which you assemble,
Fetter the demon liquor,
   And make ye the traffic tremble.

Ay! to fetter and to chain him,
   And cast him under our feet,
This is the end we aim at,
   The object for which we meet.
Then don't bring into the lodge-room,
   Envy, or strife, or pride,
Or aught that will mar our union,
   But leave them all outside.

THE MOTHER'S PRAYER.

A mother kneels by the cradle,
  Where her little infant lies,
And she sees the ghastly shadows
  Creeping around his eyes.
And she clasps her hands together,
  And her heart beats loud and wild,
And she cries in a gush of anguish,
  "O Father! save my child.

"Oh! do not, do not take him
  So soon to the home on high;
My beautiful, dark-eyed darling,
  O God! he *must not* die.
I cannot pray in meekness,
  'My Father's will be done.'
I can only cry in anguish,
  'Oh! save my infant son.'"

Slowly the ghastly shadows
  Crept from the baby's eyes,
And the mother saw the bright orbs
  Open in sweet surprise.
And she heard the lisping prattle
  And the childish laugh again,
And she clasped him close to her bosom,
  And her glad tears fell like rain.

The mother stands at the window,
  Watching the night come down,
As it settles slowly, slowly,
  Over the busy town.

And the withered face is troubled,
  And she sighs in a weary way:
"Oh! where does my darling tarry,
  Now at the close of day?

"Surely his task is ended:
  Why is it he does not come?"
Ah! mother, one word will answer,
  And that one word is Rum.
He stands at the bar this moment,
  Draining the tempter's bowl;
And your beautiful boy has entered
  His name on the drunkards' roll.

Ah! well, your prayer was answered:
  You prayed that he might not die,
That he might not join the angels
  Who dwell in their home on high.
O mother! say, is it better,
  Or is it worse than death,
To see your darling stagger,
  And feel his rum-foul breath?

You could not pray, "My Father,
  Thy will, not mine, be done,"
But cried, in your deaf, blind sorrow,
  "Oh! save my infant son."
And is he saved, fond mother?
  And which is better, pray,
To know he is there in the rum-shop,
  Or under the grass, to-day?

O God of a mighty nation!
  When shall the glad day be
That the liquor reign is ended,
  And our land is truly free?--
When our darling boys may wander
  Through all its length and breadth,
With never a serpent lurking
  To slay them in their strength?

Full many a year has vanished
  Since the grand triumphant day
When we stood in bold defiance
  Of a tyrant monarch's sway;
And now in a blood-red torrent,
  At the price of a million graves,
We have swept the bonds and shackles
  From the hands of a million slaves.

And yet we are under a tyrant,
  And yet we are slaves to-day,
And we do not bid defiance
  To the baleful liquor sway.
Up! O ye mourning captives!
  Strike at the tyrant's hand!
Loosen his hold for ever--
  Deliver a bondaged land!

THEORY AND PRACTICE.

The man of God stands, on the Sabbath-day,
Warning the sinners from the broad highway

That leads to death. He rolls his pious eye,
And tells how wily demons hidden lie
To spring upon the thoughtless souls who pass
Along. He lifts his hands, and cries, "Alas!
That such things be! O sinners! pause;
  Gird on God's armor; let the devil see
Thou hast espoused a high and holy cause,
  And all his arts are powerless on thee."

'Tis thus the man of God in warning cries,
And tears of heart-felt sorrow fill his eyes;
And then he doffs his surplice and his gown,
And calls for *wine* to wash his sorrow down.

Ah! follower of the meek and lowly One,
And is it thus that thou wouldst have men shun
The road to death? Is this the better way,
Of which thou tellest on the Sabbath-day?
This wine you sip to quench your pious thirst,
Of all the devil's arts, he reckons *first*.
And countless legions go down to the dead,
Slain soul and body by the demon red.
Is *this* the holy principle you teach?
Or shall men practise, while you only preach?

The righteous churchman reads a tale of strife,
One of those countless tragedies of city life;
He sighs, and shakes his head, and sighs again,
And thanks his God he's not as other men.
And then he sips his glass of ale or rum,
And wonders if the time shall ever come
When such things cease to be. I answer, "When
You who bear the names of Christian men

Shall with your wines, and ales, and beers dispense,
And choose the motto, 'Total Abstinence.'"

The politician sighs at the nation's debt,
And groans at his heavy tax. And yet
He calls his jolly friends from near and far,
And does not sigh or groan before the bar,
But "treats" them with a free and lavish hand,
Thus swelling the liquor tax upon the land.
And so the world goes; and will always go
As long as fools live. And their lives are long,
As all may see who look around, and so
I'll let it waggle on, and cease my song,
Hoping 'gainst hope, that some poor struggling ray
Of common sense may find its weary way
Into the stupid hearts and brains of those
Who prate of *any* evil this world knows,
And sip their wines and beer, and say to men,
"We only drink a little--now and then."

THERE'S WORK TO BE DONE.

'Tis the song of the morning,
  The words of the sun,
As he swings o'er the mountains:
  "There's work to be done:
I must wake up the sleepers,
  And banish the night;
I must paint up the heavens,
  Tuck the stars out of sight;

"Dry the dew on the meadows,
    Put warmth in the air,
Chase the fog from the lowlands,
    Stay gloom everywhere.
No pausing, no resting,
    There's work to be done.
It is upward and onward,
    Still on," says the sun.

'Tis the song of our soldiers
    Who bravely march on:
"There are souls to be gathered,
    There's work to be done:
We must wake up the sleepers,
    And teach them to *think*;
We must paint in full horrors
    The breakers of *drink*;

"Dry the tears of the mourners,
    Put the cups out of sight,
And, Eastward and Westward,
    Proclaim, 'There is light.'
'Tis the Marseillaise of Progress--
    There's work to be done,"
The song of our soldiers,
    The song of the sun.

THE TEMPERANCE ARMY.

Though you see no banded army,
    Though you hear no cannons rattle,

We are in a mighty contest,
  We are fighting a great battle.
    We are few, but we are right:
    And we wage the holy fight,
    Night and day, and day and night.

If we do not fail or falter,
  If we do not sleep or slumber,
We shall win in this great contest,
  Though the foe is twice our number.
    This the burden of our song,
    "We are few, but we are strong,
    And right *must* triumph over wrong."

O my sisters! O my brothers!
  There is death all round about us.
Must we, then, sit down discouraged?
  Will you let the wine-cup rout us?
    Hear the drunkard's awful wail!
    See the mourners, bowed and pale!
    Will you, coward, then say "fail"?

Say not that your heart is with us
  When you do not help or aid us.
All who love the cause sincerely
  Can do something: God has made us
    Tongues to talk with: you can say
    Something, if you will, each day,
    That will help us on our way,

Though you are not highly gifted,
  Though you are not bard or poet,
Though you cannot preach or lecture,

You can love the cause, and show it
  Boldly, in each thing you do.
  Seeking all that's pure and true,
  This will be a help from you.

You can say the liquor traffic
  Is a curse to any nation;
You can say that prohibition
  Is a blessing and salvation.
    You can sow good seeds, and, though
    You may never see them grow,
    They will not be lost, I know.

In this mighty temperance contest,
  Where no guns or cannons rattle,
Though you cannot lead the army
  Or be chieftain of the battle,
    With that mighty sword, the *tongue*,
    You can fight against the wrong,
    You can sing some temperance song.

Say not that you cannot aid us!
  Drops of water make the river--
Make the mighty Mississippi,
  That flows on hand on for ever.
    Every word you say for *Right*
    Gives us courage, gives us might,
    And brings nearer, morn and night.

THE TWO ARMIES.

Once over the ocean in distant lands,
In an age long past, were two hostile bands--
Two armies of men, both brave, both strong,
And their hearts beat high as they marched along
To fight the battle of right and wrong.

Never, I think, did the Eye of heaven
Look down on two armies so nearly even
In well-trained soldiers, in strength and might.
But one was the *Wrong*, and one was the *Right*,
And the last was the stronger in heaven's sight.
And these hostile armies drew near, one night,
And pitched their tents on two hill-sides green,
With only the brow of a hill between.

With the first red beams of the morning light
Both knew would open the awful fight,
And one of the armies lay hushed and still,
And slept in the tents on the green side-hill.
Heart beat with heart: and they all were as one
In the thought of the battle to be begun
With the first bright glance of the morning sun.
Their aim was ignoble, their cause was wrong,
But they were *united*, and so they were strong.

Not so the army just over the hill:
While the ranks of the foe were hushed and still,
The ranks of the *Right* were torn with strife,
And with noise and confusion the air was rife.

Disputes and quarrels, dissensions and jars,
And the sound of fighting, and civil wars;

And, ere the morning, brother and brother,
Instead of the enemy, fought with each other.

Over the hill, the foe, in glee,
Listened and laughed. "Ho ho!" quoth he.
"There is strife in the enemy's ranks, I see,
And the bright red beams of the rising sun
Will see a victory easily won.
It matters little how strong the foe,
This is a truth we all do know:
There is no success without unity,
However noble the cause may be.
The day is ours before it's begun.
Ho! for the triumph so easily won."

And on the morrow, the ranks of the Right
Were routed and beaten, and put to flight,
And the Wrong was the victor, and gained the fight.

There are two armies abroad to-day,
As in the age that has passed away.

The makers, and venders, and patrons, and all
Who aid in the traffic of Alcohol,
These are the warriors, bold and strong,
Who swell the ranks of the army of Wrong.
And we are the soldiers, true and brave,
Who are striving with heart and hand to save
The youths of our land from the deep, dark grave
That the foe is digging by day and by night.
Only *one thing* can defeat the Right.
There is nothing *but* triumph for us, unless
Dissension, that crafty foe to success,

Creeps into our ranks. Oh! let us *unite*!
Let heart beat with heart as we enter the fight;
Let the whole mighty army be *one* for the time,
And sweep on the foe in a column sublime
In its unity, earnestness, oneness, and might,
Till the foe stands aghast at the wonderful sight,
Till the enemy cowers and shivers, afraid
Of the awful approach of the grand cavalcade.
Close up the ranks, brothers! sisters, draw near,
We are fighting one fight, we are all kinsmen here.
Closer, still closer! in nearness lies might.
Love is our watchword--on to the fight!

THE TWO SHIPS.

On the sea of life they floated,
  Brothers twain in manhood's pride,
And the good ship "Temperance" bore them,
  Safely o'er the stormy tide.
Not a thought of rock or breaker,
  Not a fear of wreck had they,
For their ship was strong and steady--
  Faithful, trusty, night and day.

So they floated on together,
  Full of youth's elastic joy,
Floated till the air was startled
  With the cry of "Boat ahoy!"
And they saw a craft beside them,
  Dainty, jaunty, frail, and fair,

And its banner showed a wine-glass,
   Painted as its symbol there.

And again the stranger shouted,
   "Boat ahoy! a friend is near!
Captain of yon gallant vessel,
   Do you see, and do you hear?
We're the 'Social Glass,' my hearties,
   And a jolly, jovial crew.
We are bound for Pleasure Valley,
   And we would be friends with you."

But the brothers stood in silence,
   Though they could not help but hear,
And the elder's heart was throbbing
   With a vague and chilling fear.
And again the stranger pleaded,
   "Come aboard the 'Social Glass'!
We will entertain you warmly,
   And the time will quickly pass."

Still the elder stood unheeding,
   Still he did not move or turn,
And his mien was cold and haughty,
   And his face was dark and stern.
But the younger whispered to him,
   "Surely, we are churls to stand
In this sullen, boorish silence;
   Let us offer friendship's hand.

"See! they beckon us to join them!
   Beckon us with word and smile.
I will not refuse them longer,

I will join them for a while."
Then the "Social Glass" rowed nearer,
   And he joined the jovial throng,
And they gathered round about him,
   Greeting him with laugh and song.

Then the elder cried in anguish,
   Loud and wild his accents fell:
"Know you not, O brother, brother!
   Yonder ship is bound for hell?
See the clouds that hover o'er you!
   And the day is growing dark:
There is ruin and destruction
   For each soul upon that bark.

"Oh! come back! Why did you leave me?
   It is certain death to stay,
Do not loiter! do not linger!
   Brother, brother, come away!"
But the wild winds only answered
   To his agonizing plea;
And the "Social Glass" went bounding
   Lightly o'er the troubled sea.

He could hear their shouts of laughter,
   He could see their goblets shine,
He could see his darling brother
   With his lips all red with wine.
Ah! a seething, boiling maelstrom
   Lay within their very track,
And he warned them of their danger,
   And he strove to turn them back.

But they did not, would not heed him:
  On they went in wildest glee!
Nearer, nearer to the whirlpool,
  Nearer to the boiling sea,
Till the "Social Glass" was buried
  In the seething, rushing wave,
And each mad and wreckless voyager
  Found a dark and awful grave.

And the lonely brother floated
  Calmly o'er the stormy tide,
For the good ship "Temperance" bore him
  Safely o'er the waters wide.
And he never left her shelter
  Till the voyage of life was o'er,
And he anchored where the angels
  Waited for him on the shore.

WERE I MAN GROWN.

Were I man grown, I'd stand
With clean heart, soul, and hand,
An honor to this land.

I would be good and true.
I would not *smoke* and *chew*
As many grown men do.

Tobacco is foul stuff.
Hogs root it from the trough,
And serve it right enough.

I wish I'd every seed
And plant of that bad weed,
I'd make a fire indeed!

And these two lips of mine
Should never *taste* of *wine*,
Though it might glow and shine.

No wine, no beer, no gin,
No ale, no rum--within
Each drink lurk shame and sin.

And I'd not swear. Ah! when
We boys grow into men,
You'll see true manhood then.

For we shall be and do
Just what I've said; and you
Had better try it, too.

WHAT HAD HE DONE?

I saw the farmer, when the day was done,
  And the proud sun had sought his crimson bed,
And the mild stars came forward one by one--
  I saw the sturdy farmer, and I said:
    "What have you done to-day,
    O farmer! say?"

"Oh! I have sown the wheat in yonder field,
And pruned my orchard to increase its yield,

And turned the furrow for a patch of corn:
This have I done, with other things, since morn."

I saw the blacksmith in his smithy-door,
  When day had vanished and the west grew red,
And all the busy noise and strife were o'er--
  I saw the kingly blacksmith, and I said:
    "What have you done to-day,
    O blacksmith! say?

"Oh! I have made two plough-shares all complete,
And nailed the shoes on many horses' feet;
And--O my friend! I cannot tell you half,"
The man of muscle answered, with a laugh.

I saw the miller, when the day had gone,
  And all the sunlight from the hills had fled,
And tender shadows crept across the lawn--
  I saw the trusty miller, and I said:
    "What have you done to-day,
    O miller gray?"

"Oh! I have watched my mill from morn to night,
And never saw yon flour so snowy white.
And many are the mouths to-day I've fed,
I ween," the merry miller laughed and said.

I saw another, when the night grew nigh,
  And turned each daily toiler from his task,
When gold and crimson banners decked the sky--
  I saw another, and I paused to ask:
    "What have you done to-day,
    Rumseller, say?"

But the rumseller turned with dropping head,
And not a single word in answer said.
What had he done? His work he knew full well
Was plunging human souls in deepest hell.

Alas! rumseller, on that awful day,
  When death shall call you, and your race is run,
How can you answer? What can you hope to say?
  When God shall ask you, "What have you done?"
    How can you meet the eye
    Of the Most High?

When night approaches and the day grows late,
Think you to find the way to heaven's gate?
Think you to dwell with souls of righteous men?
Think you to enter in? If not, what then?

WHAT I HAVE SEEN.

NUMBER I.

I saw a mother give wine to her boy--
  The rain-drops fall and fall:
The pride of his parents, a household joy,
  A mother's blessing, her all.

I saw the cheek of the youth grow red--
  The rain falls over the lea:
The light of his eye shone like jewels, they said:
  It spoke of ruin to me.

I saw the youth drink again and again--
  The rain falls heavy and fast:
I saw the mother's brow furrowed with pain,
  She was reaping her harvest at last.

I saw the youth go staggering by--
  The rain-drops beat and beat:
Dulled was the light of his beautiful eye;
  I saw him fall in the street.

I heard the rabble cry, "Shame! oh! shame!"
  The rain-drops sob and sob:
I heard the drunkard's once-honored name
  Shouted aloud by the mob.

I saw the youth carried home to his door--
  The rain-drops sob and sigh:
Saw the friends shun him, who sought him before,
  Saw him sink lower, and die.

I saw the stone that bore only his name--
  The rain-drops mutter and rave:
I saw the mother with sorrow and shame
  Bowed to the brink of the grave.

WHAT I HAVE SEEN.

NUMBER II.

I saw a maid with her chivalrous lover:
  He was both tender and true;
He kissed her lips, vowing over and over,

"Darling, I worship you."
Sing, sing, bird of the spring,
Tell of the flowers the summer will bring.

I saw the maiden, sweet, loving, confiding,
  Smile when he whispered "Mine,"
Saw her lips meet his with no word of chiding,
  Though his breath fumed with wine.
Wail, wail, Nightingale,
Sing of a mourner bowed and pale.

I saw the lover and maid at the altar,
  Bound by the bands divine;
Heard the responses--they fail not nor falter--
  Saw the guests pledge in wine.
Howl, howl, ominous Owl,
Shriek of the terrible tempest's scowl.

I saw the drunkard's wife weeping in anguish,
  Saw her struck down by a blow;
I saw the husband in prison-cells languish--
  Thus ends the tale of woe.
Shriek, shriek, O Raven! speak
Of the terrible midnight, dark and bleak.

WHAT I HAVE SEEN.

NUMBER III.

I saw two youths: both were fair in the face,
They had set out foot to foot in life's race;
But one said to the other, "I say now, my brother,

You are going a little too slow;
The world will look on, and say, 'See Josy John,'
    We must put on more style, now, you know."

So he tipped a plug hat on one side of his pate,
And strutted along with a Jockey Club gait;
And he carried a cane, and said, "It is plain,
    I am too fine a fellow to toil.
I can gamble and bet, and a good living get;
    But my hands are too pretty to soil.

"My friend in the rear, you are slow, I am fast;
I am up with the times--I am first, you are last.
So I guess I will leave you--aw, if it won't grieve
you;
    I'll wait for you when I get through;
Or, when up on the hill, I'll remem-bah you still,
    And--aw, mayhap I'll come and help you."

I saw him pass on with a strut through the street;
Saw him stopped by a score of "good boys" for a
treat.
While the calm "Josy John" went quietly on,
    And kept his lips free from the bowl;
Worked at whatever came, turned from sin and
from shame,
    And wrote "Purity," "Truth," in his soul.

I saw two men: one was fair to behold;
The other, a drunken sot, bloated and bold.
One stood on the mountain and drank of God's
fountain,
    The other drank beer in the street.

Yet both started alike; but one made a "strike,"
Which ended, you see, in defeat.

WHAT I HAVE SEEN.

NUMBER IV.

I saw a youth, one of God's favored few,
    Crowned with beauty, and talents, and health;
He had climbed the steep pathway, and cut his way
through
    To the summit of glory and wealth.
The day is breaking, hearts are waking,
    Refreshed for the field of labor:
Arise, arise, like the king of the skies,
    With a greeting for friend and neighbor.

He had toiled hard for the honors he'd won,
    He had climbed over high rocks, forded streams;
Braved the bleak winter snow, the hot summer sun,
    He was reaching the goal of his dreams.
The day hangs around us, the sun hath bound us
    With fetters silken and yellow:
Flow, flow away, fleeting day,
    Golden-hearted and mellow.

I saw the youth lift a mug to his mouth,
    Drink the last drop of the fearful *first glass*!
Ah! his veins thrill in a fierce, scorching drouth,
    He fills it again, again drinks it! alas!
The day is dying, hearts are sighing,
    Crushed with a weight of sorrow:

Sleep, oh! sleep, in a slumber deep,
  And wait for a bright to-morrow.

I saw him low in the dust at my feet,
  Gone beauty, health, wealth, strength, talents, *all*;
From the summit of Fame to the slime of the street,
  He had bartered his soul for the fiend Alcohol.
The night hangs o'er us, the wind's wild chorus
  Shrieks like a demons' revel:
Weep, sob, weep, for the fog is deep,
  And the world is sold to the devil.

WHAT I HAVE SEEN.

NUMBER V.

I saw a Christian, a temperance man,
  Casting his ballot one day at the polls:
One who believes he does what he can
  Toward the reclaiming and saving of souls.
    And may be he does--may be he does!
    I don't say he *doesn't*, but *may be* he does!

I saw his candidate sipping his beer,
  Wiping his moustache and lapping his jaws;
And I said to myself, "It's decidedly queer,
  If this is the man that should help make our laws."
    But may be he is--may be he is!
    I won't say it outright, but *may be* he is!

I saw an old drunkard fall in the street:
  I saw my Christian man mournfully pass,

And mournfully say to the sot at his feet:
  "I have done what I could for such wrecks, but,
alas!"
    Well, may be he had--may be he had!
    I don't say he *hadn't*, but may be he had!

I know a party that's forming to-day,
  Made out of men that are loyal and brave:
They will sweep liquor taxes and tariffs away,
  For they never will vote for a drinking old knave.
    You see if they do! you see if they do!
    I don't say I *know*, but *you see* if they do!

WHAT WE WANT.

We have scores of temperance men,
  Bold and earnest, brave and true,
Fighting with the tongue and pen,
  And we value what they do.
    But, my friends,
    To gain our ends,
  You must use the ballot, too.

When we tell about our cause,
  Politicians only smile;
While they mould and make our laws,
  What care they for rank or file?
    "Preach and pray,"
    They sneer and say;
  "We'll make liquor laws the while."

We want men who dare to fling
  Party ties and bonds away;
Who will cast them off, and cling
  To the RIGHT, and boldly say,
    "No beer bloats
    Shall get our votes."
  Then shall our cause gain the day.

WHERE ARE THE TEMPERANCE PEOPLE?

IN REPLY TO A QUERY

Where are the temperance people?
  Well, scattered here and there:
Some gathering in their produce
  To show at the autumn fair;
Some threshing wheat for market,
  And others threshing rye,
That will go to the fat distiller
  For whiskey by-and-by.

And some are selling their hop crops
  At a first-rate price, this year,
And the seller pockets the money,
  While the drunkard swallows the beer.
And some "staunch temperance workers"(?)
  Who'd do anything for the cause,
Save to give it a dime or a moment,
  Or work for temperance laws,

May be seen from now to election,
   Near any tavern stand
Where liquor flows in plenty,
   With a voter on either hand.
And these temperance office-seekers
   That we hear of far and near
Are the ones who furnish the money
   That buys the lager-beer.

But these are only the black sheep
   Who want the temperance name
Without living up to the precepts,
   And so bring themselves to shame.
And the true, brave temperance people,
   Who have the cause at heart,
Are doing the work that's nearest,
   Each his allotted part:

Some lifting the fallen drunkard,
   Some preaching unto men,
Some aiding the cause with money,
   And others with the pen.
Each has a different mission,
   Each works in a different way,
But their works shall melt together
   In one grand result, some day.

And one, our chief (God bless him),
   Is working day and night:
With his sword of burning eloquence,
   He is fighting the noble fight.
Whether in lodge or convention,
   Whether at home or abroad,

He is reaping a golden harvest
  To lay at the feet of God.

Where are the temperance people?
  All scattered here and there,
Sowing the seeds of righteous deeds,
That the harvest may be fair.

"WHERE IS THY BROTHER?"

Oh! when I think in what a thorny way
The feet of men must ever walk and stray,
I do not wonder that so many fall,
But wonder more that any stand at all.

I look around me, and on every hand
I see the palaces of destruction stand
Like whited sepulchres: some seem to be
All white and clean, and pure as purity.

I see a path of flowers, blooming fair,
But, oh! a dark abyss is hidden there.
I see a serpent lurking in the grass
Where manly feet will all unheeding pass.

I see the maiden with the beaming eye,
She lightly laughs and lifts the wine-glass high,
And says the while her red lips sip and taste,
"A fig for temperance; wine is too good to waste."

It is so hard for men to walk within
The narrow path that leads away from sin;
So hard to keep unto the better way,
Even with woman's hand to guide alway;

But when she scorns and jeers the noble strife,
And turns them from the higher, better life,
And leads them downward with her own fair hand,
Oh! can we wonder that they do not stand?

Alas! my sisters, I can only pray,
May God forgive you on the judgment-day;
"Where is thy brother, where?" the Master saith,
And you, like Cain, must answer for his death.

WILD OATS.

I saw a fair youth, with a brow broad and white,
And an eye that was beaming with intellect's light:
And his face seemed to glow with the wealth of his
mind;
And I said, "He will grace and ennoble mankind:
  He is Nature's own king."

We met yet again. I saw the youth stand
With a bowl that was flowing and red in his hand;
And he filled it again, and again did he quaff,
And his friends gathered round him, and said with a
laugh,
  "He is sowing his oats."

Ah! his eye was too bright, and his cheek was too
red,
And I gazed on the youth with a feeling of dread;
And again as he laughingly lifted the bowl,
I turned from the scene with a shuddering soul:
   It was terrible seed!

We met but once more. I found in the street
A corpse half-enveloped in mud and in sleet:
A foul, bloated thing; but I saw in the face
A something that told of its boyhood's grace:
   He had reaped the dire crop.

O youths who are sowing wild oats! do you know
That the terrible seed you are planting will grow?
Have you thought how your God will require some
day
An account of the life you are throwing away?
   Have you thought, O rash youth?

It will soon be too late, there is no time to waste;
Then throw down the cup! do not touch, do not
taste!
It is filled with destruction and sorrow and pain:
Throw it down! throw it down! do not lift it again:
   It will soon be too late!

WORDS FROM THE WIND.

I called to the wind of the Winter,
   As he sped like a steed on his way,

"Oh! rest for awhile on thy journey,
   And answer these questions, I pray.

"Who is the foe to all virtue,
   Who is the chieftain of crime?
Who blackens the forehead of beauty,
   And cheateth the finger of time?
Who maketh the heart to be aged,
   In the beautiful morning of youth?
Who is the herald of sorrow,
   And who the assassin of Truth?
Who is the help-meet of Satan,
   The agent of regions below?
Who the promoter of vices?
   Who loadeth the bosom with woe?
Who stealeth the strength of the mighty?
   Who stealeth the wits of the wise?
Who maketh the good and the noble
   A thing that the meanest despise?"

And the wind of the wild Winter answered,
   In a voice like a clarion call:
"'Tis a beast legion-headed, a demon
   Whom men christened 'King Alcohol.'
This is the help-meet that Satan
   Sends out from the kingdom of hell,
A many-faced demon, who doeth
   The work of the master right well;
For he weaveth his web round the noble,
   And slayeth the soul with his breath.
Ah! this is the foe to all virtue,
   And this is the agent of death."

WORK FOR WOMAN.

Woman, sitting at your ease,
In the midst of luxuries,
Bound by chains of selfishness,
With no aim but "how to dress,"
Does the thought ne'er come to you
Of the thing that you could do?
    Could, and yet do not,
To crush out the liquor trade,
That is making, and has made,
Sin and shame, and woe and tears
In our land, for years and years--
    Have you never thought?

You will chat for hours and hours
Over ribbons, silks, and flowers,
But you will not talk or think
Of this growing evil--drink.
You will weep and smile and laugh
Over trashy books of chaff,
    But you will not read
Any truthful temperance tale.
"They are all so dry and stale--
Just the same old thing," you say
As you yawn, and turn away
    From the truths you need.

You have time for rout, and ball,
Concert, theatre, and all
Lectures, save on this one theme.
"Oh! these temperance lectures seem
So extremely dull," you cry,

93

With a listless air and eye.
    O my friend! forsake
That absorbing theme of DRESS,
Drop for once your selfishness,
Think of all there is to do!
See the work that waits for you!
    Up! arouse! awake!

There are men for you to save
From the wretched drunkard's grave.
There are feet that strayed away
Into paths of sin one day.
You can bring them, if you will,
To the paths upon the hill.
    There's enough to do!
There's much to do and little done,
Women, sisters, every one,
Lend a helping hand, nor shirk
Any part of God's great work.
    Come! we've need of you!

Drops of Water: Poems by Ella Wheeler
New York : The National Temperance Society and
Publication House, 1872.

Printed in the United States
143594LV00002B/67/A

9 781417 969685